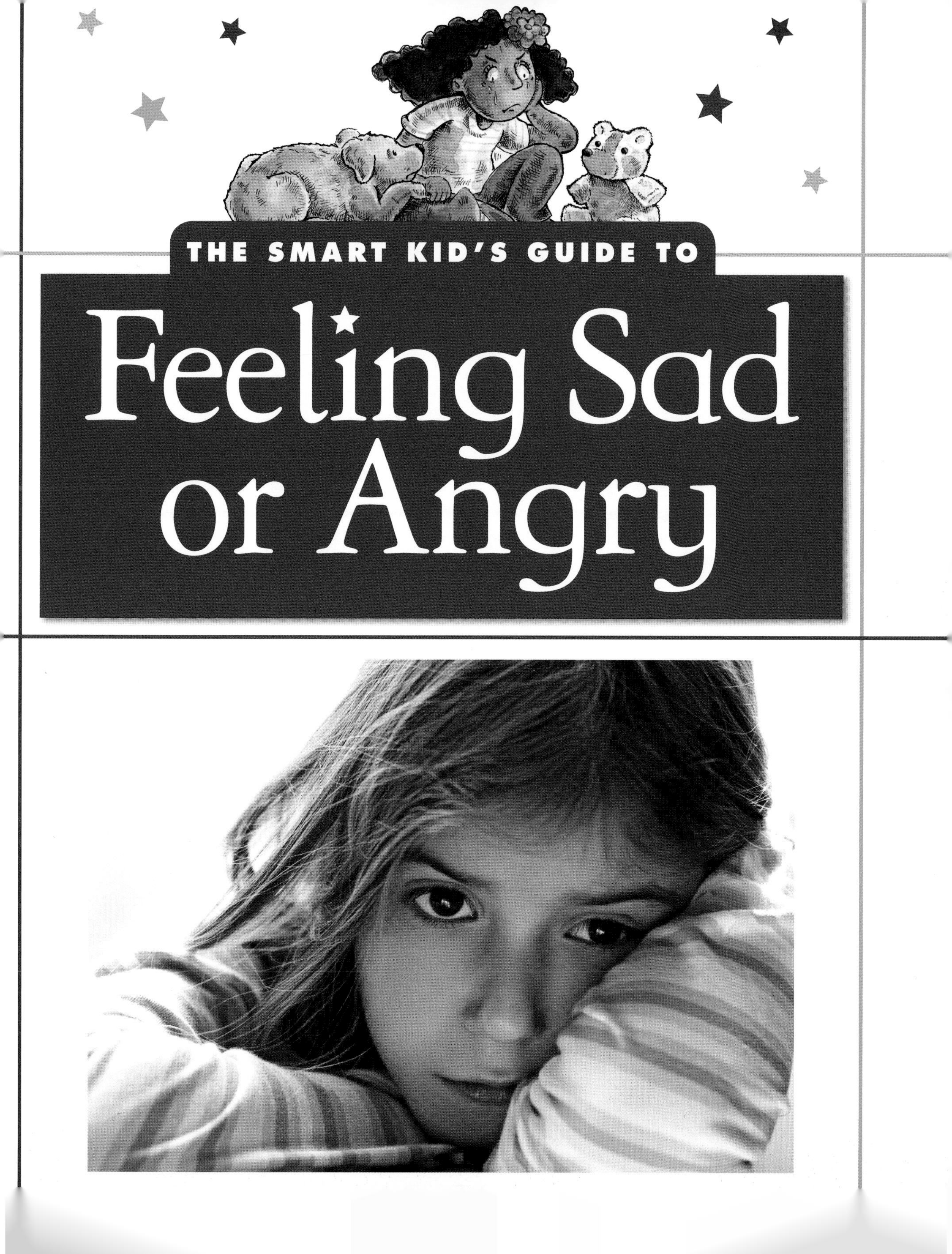

THE SMART KID'S GUIDE TO

Feeling Sad or Angry

Published by The Child's World®
1980 Lookout Drive • Mankato, MN 56003-1705
800-599-READ • www.childsworld.com

Acknowledgments
The Child's World®: Mary Berendes, Publishing Director
Content Adviser: Philip C. Rodkin, Professor of Child Development, Departments of Educational Psychology and Psychology, University of Illinois
The Design Lab: Design
Red Line Editorial: Editorial Direction
Amnet: Production

Photographs © Shutterstock Images, cover, 1, 7, 13, 15, 18 (left), 18 (right), 26, 29; Belinda Pretorius/Shutterstock Images, 5; Rob Marmion/Shutterstock Images, 6; Michael C. Gray/Shutterstock Images, 9; Ints Vikmanis/Shutterstock Images, 11; Margot Petrowski/Shutterstock Images, 12; Natalia Sannikova/Shutterstock Images, 16; Mandy Godbehear/Shutterstock Images, 17; Nolte Lourens/Shutterstock Images, 21; Guryanov Andrey/Shutterstock Images, 22, 23; Ingrid Balabanova/Shutterstock Images, 24; Robert Hoetink/Shutterstock Images, 27; Stephen Coburn/Shutterstock Images, 28

ISBN 9781626873414
LCCN 2014930679

Printed in the United States of America
Mankato, MN
July, 2014
PA02224

ABOUT THE AUTHOR

M. J. Cosson was born in Des Moines, Iowa. She has been a teacher, writer, editor, and artist. She is a court-appointed special advocate for children in foster care. She has five grandchildren and lives in the Texas hill country with her husband and pets.

ABOUT THE ILLUSTRATOR

Ronnie Rooney took art classes constantly as a child. She was always drawing and painting at her mom's kitchen table. She got her BFA in painting from the University of Massachusetts at Amherst and her MFA in illustration from the Savannah College of Art and Design in Savannah, Georgia. Ronnie lives on a U.S. Army base with her infantryman husband and two small children. Ronnie hopes to pass on her love of art and sports to her kids.

CONTENTS

CHAPTER 1

What Are Anger and Sadness?

Everybody feels bad sometimes. Understanding what you are feeling will help you know how to deal with it.

Sadness is a feeling of **grief** or unhappiness. If you feel sad you might not feel liked by friends.

You might not feel loved. Sadness can come because you do not feel good about yourself. A disappointment can make you feel sad. There are many causes for sadness.

Sadness can feel like a burning behind your eyes. You might need to cry. Or sadness might feel like a hole in your heart. You might want to be alone. You can be a little sad or very sad. The feeling of sadness can travel through your whole body. You might feel like you have no energy. Sadness can make you want to curl up into a ball and hide.

Sometimes sadness is called "feeling blue."

You might feel angry if you are fighting with a friend or family member.

Anger is a feeling of being annoyed or upset. Anger may be a reaction to a threat. You might feel angry if someone takes something from you. You might get angry if someone calls you a mean name. Or maybe you think something unfair happened to you. You can be a little angry or very angry. When you are just a little angry, you might say that you are **irritated**. If you are very angry you might call it **rage**. Your brain is thinking only of anger. You might act without thinking first.

Anger can begin the same way sadness does. It can feel like a burning behind your eyes. Your throat might feel tight. Your heart might start beating fast. You might begin to breathe fast. Anger can make you want to scream or hit something.

Anger might make you want to scream.

Read each line below. Think about whether it would make you feel sad or angry. Maybe you would feel both sad and angry.

- *You lost something.*
- *You fought with a friend.*
- *You have nothing to do.*
- *Your feelings have been hurt.*
- *You are sick.*
- *You are worried.*
- *You have been hurt.*
- *You can't go out to play.*
- *You have to do something you don't want to do.*
- *You are tired.*
- *You made a mistake.*
- *You are being* **ignored** *by somebody.*
- *Someone near you feels bad.*
- *You watched a television show that made you feel bad.*
- *You just want to kick something.*
- *You are confused.*

When was the last time you felt angry? Do you know why you felt angry? When did you last feel sad? Do you know why you felt sad? What did you do when you had these feelings? Knowing how you felt and remembering how you acted can help you learn how to deal with these feelings when they come again.

Keep a vocabulary list of words that are feelings. When you learn a new word, add it to your list. Write a definition for it. The next time you have a strong feeling, look at your list afterward. Decide which feeling you felt. You might want to write about what happened and how you felt. You also might want to add to your definition or change it.

CHAPTER 2

Everyone Feels Anger and Sadness

Both sadness and anger are natural feelings. Your body needs to let these feelings happen. It is healthy to let them happen. But it is important to learn how to deal with them when they do happen.

It is okay to feel sad once in a while. You might need to cry. Feeling sad for a bit helps your

Everyone feels angry sometimes.

body get rid of **stress**. Sadness is natural. Tears can be good.

It is okay to feel angry from time to time. Anger can come quickly. It is a natural defense when you feel a threat. Sometimes anger comes because you have had all you can take. Something needs to change.

Life is always changing. Your feelings change, too. Feelings of anger and sadness will pass in time.

Sometimes you don't know why you feel sad or angry.

Often anger or sadness comes because something happened. You are **reacting** to something that upset you.

Sometimes bad feelings just come to you. Someone close to you might notice and ask if you got up on the wrong side of the bed. That means that you are acting sad or angry. You might not know what made you feel that way. Perhaps you had a bad dream. Maybe you watched a scary show. You might have eaten something before you went to bed that made you have a restless night. All kinds of small things can change the way you feel.

Sometimes you feel angry because someone around you is acting angry. You might feel sad because someone near you feels sad a lot. How people around you deal with bad feelings can affect how you deal with them.

You might feel sad or angry because the people around you feel that way.

CHAPTER 3

Learning to Handle Anger and Sadness

Babies can't do things for themselves, so they cry. It is their way of getting people to feed them and care for them. Toddlers and preschoolers sometimes have **tantrums**. They haven't learned the skills or words to deal with their needs. They become angry and lose control.

Growing up takes a lot of work. You are learning many new things. You are learning to read, write, and think. You are learning math, science, and history. You are learning other things, too. You don't have a special class to teach you how to handle your feelings. But the adults in your life are teaching you those lessons all the time.

Babies and toddlers cry to get what they need.

Part of growing up is learning to understand your feelings.

You are learning **coping skills** for different **emotions**. Part of the hard work of growing up is learning to take charge of yourself. When you leave home as an adult, you will need to know how to get a job. You will need to know how to cook a meal. You will need to know how to handle money. You will need to be able to take care of yourself. Part of growing up is understanding how you feel and knowing what to do about it.

You can begin to learn ways to deal with anger and sadness. You can learn ways to cope with bad feelings.

A good way to understand something is to act it out. Try it with an older person or a good friend. Think of something that would make you angry. Let's say that a bully just tripped you. You fell to the ground. You are embarrassed. Your knees hurt. And you want to fight! Act out what you would do. Would you fight? Then think of a better choice. Are there more appropriate ways to show your anger? Role-play about feeling sad, too.

Happiness, sadness, and anger are all part of life.

Imagine how life would be if you didn't have feelings. Have you ever heard anyone say that you have to take the bad with the good? Joy, happiness, **contentment**, and all good feelings are part of life. When you feel these feelings, life is brighter. You enjoy what you are doing.

To live a full life, you get a little anger and sadness, too. What matters is how you deal with them. These feelings can be harmful if they come too often or last too long.

Sadness that lasts too long is not good for you. It can make you forget about things you need to do. It can even make you feel sick.

Anger that you can't control is not good for you or others. Being angry can stop you in your tracks. You can get so upset that you can't do anything else. Or you might say unkind things you don't really mean. You might want to hurt yourself or someone else. It can make you feel sick, too.

If you find that you always feel a little gloomy or mad, you can get help. Tell a parent, a teacher, or someone else at school. No one should have to spend too much time being sad or angry. Trusted adults can help you deal with these feelings.

CHAPTER 4

What You Can Do to Feel Better

The first thing you need to do when you feel sad or angry is to recognize your feeling. You need to know it's happening to you. If you can, think about why it is happening. You might have to put up with the bad feeling for a while. There are real reasons to be upset. You cannot ignore them.

Once you have begun to sort through the problem, you can start to move on. You can do many things to help yourself get past sadness and anger. The next time you feel sad or angry, try one of these tips to feel better.

Smiling can make you and others feel better. Try it. Look at someone. First smile with your eyes. Then put a big grin on your face. Most of the time, the other person will smile back. Now think about how you feel inside. This is a great exercise when you feel just a little sad.

Exercise can help you feel better. Get off the couch and go outside. Take some deep breaths and enjoy the fresh air. Take a little run or a fast walk. Play some basketball. Hit a few baseballs. Jump rope. Play tag with someone. If the weather is bad, do some jumping jacks or stretches and bends. Get your heart pumping.

Here are some yoga moves that can help you feel better. Child's pose—Sit back on your knees with your feet about hip width under you. Bend at the waist until your forehead touches the floor. Bring your arms alongside you. You can also stretch your arms out on the floor in front of you. Remember to take long, deep breaths.

Yoga is calming. Take long, slow, deep breaths. Breathe in peace and joy. Breathe out sadness and anger.

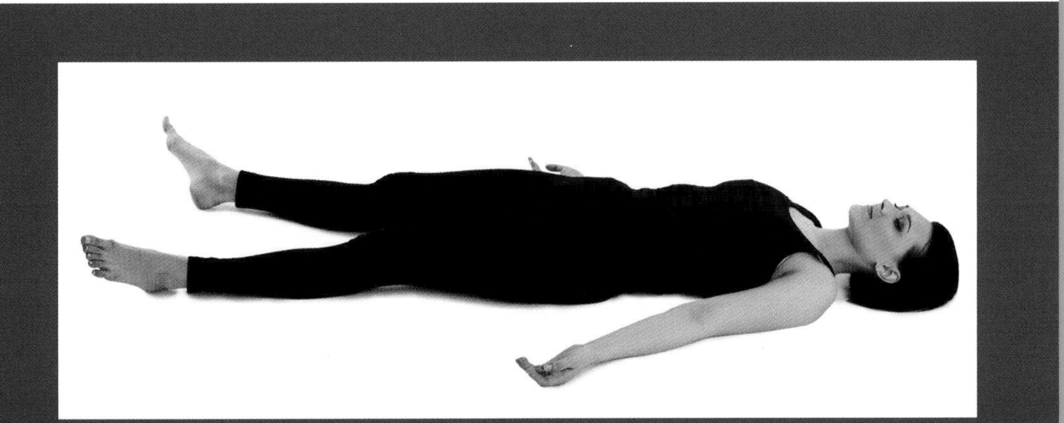

Relax pose—Lie on your back. Put your arms out straight and slightly away from your body with your palms up. Close your eyes. Make fists and scrunch up your face. Tighten every muscle in your body. Tighten your legs and arms so much that they lift off the floor a little. Count to five. Then relax. Try to make your body sink into the floor. This is good to do right before you go to sleep.

Look for good **role models**. Search out adults you like. Watch how they act. How do they handle their feelings? What do they do when they are angry or sad? Try to act like they do.

Practice peaceful **resolution**. If you feel bad and someone else is involved, talk to the person. Try to see the other person's point of view. Maybe there was a misunderstanding. Maybe you were

If you want to cheer up, try doing something fun!

both too pushy. You might need to tell that person that you are sorry. Or you might need to tell the person why you feel bad. For this kind of talk you might need the help of a teacher, parent, or school counselor.

Write in a journal. Writing in a journal is kind of like talking to yourself. A journal is not meant for others to read. It is a place to put your feelings.

Doing something you like can help bad feelings pass. Try doing something you love, even if you don't feel like it. Do you like to bake cookies? Go hiking outside? Play soccer? Draw? Make things from clay? Sometimes when you are sad, doing something you enjoy—especially something messy—can cheer you up.

Sometimes talking to a parent or trusted adult can help you work out your feelings.

Talk with someone. Choose a parent, teacher, counselor, or another adult you know. An adult usually has more experience with feelings and might be able to help you. Sometimes, though, just talking to someone can make you feel better.

Take a minute to think about all the good people and things in your life. These might include family members, friends, pets, sports, hobbies, good times you've had, favorite toys, and books. Think about why you are thankful for each one.

Hug somebody. Hugging can make you feel better. Pet a dog or cat or stuffed animal.

Have a good cry. Crying is helpful. It can get rid of stress. It can help you breathe easier. Crying when you are upset can calm you down.

Sometimes you just need to cry and let your feelings out.

Feelings of anger and sadness will pass.

Everyone feels sad sometimes. Everyone gets angry, too. These feelings are natural. Sometimes you need to feel sad or mad. These feelings help you deal with what is happening in your life.

Learn to recognize these feelings when you feel them. Practice coping skills. Have a good cry, or ask someone for a hug.

Know that the feeling is temporary. Life is constantly changing. You might need to experience sadness or anger. Life will go on. You will feel better again.

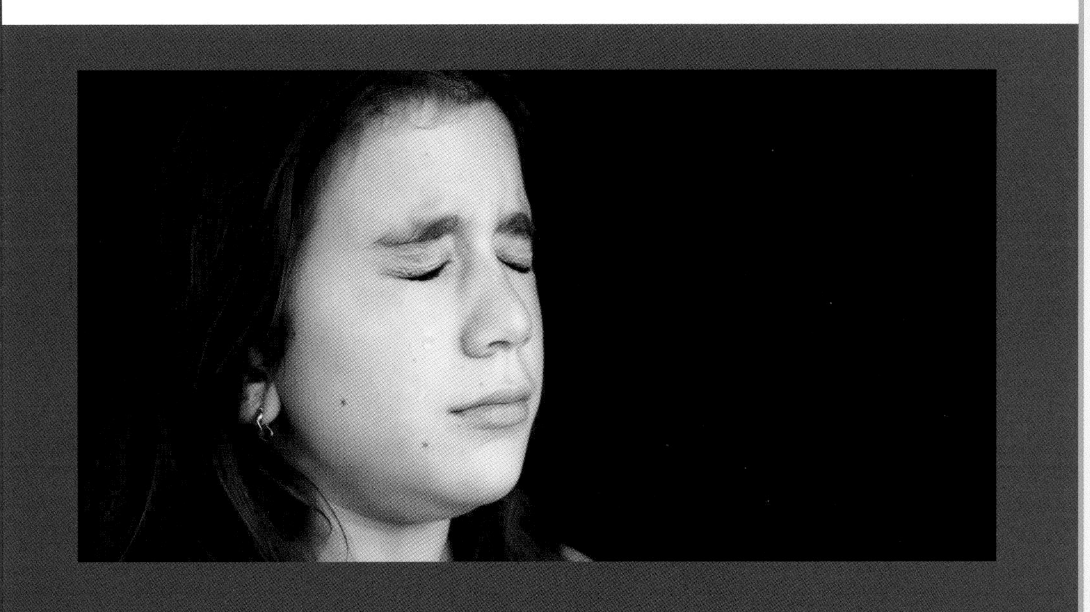

When you feel yourself getting angry, try to become a hermit crab. Take a couple of big, deep breaths. Picture yourself going into your shell. It's your way of giving yourself a time-out. You might want to go into a quiet room alone, sit down, and close your eyes. Think of yourself in the shell. Take more deep breaths. As you relax a little, try to think of solutions. Can you talk it out? Can you let it go? Maybe you need to ask an adult for help. When you feel calm, come out of your shell. Continue to work on solving your problem. You might feel better already because you took care of yourself.

TOP TEN THINGS TO KNOW

1. Being sad or angry will not last.
2. Become a hermit crab.
3. Write in a journal or do something you like.
4. Smile.
5. Exercise.
6. Cry.
7. Hug somebody or pet a pet.
8. Try peaceful resolution—talk with the person you are having problems with.
9. Find a good role model to learn from.
10. If you cannot shake being sad or angry, ask a trusted adult for help.

GLOSSARY

contentment (kuhn-TENT-muhnt) Contentment is feeling free from worry. Feelings of contentment are peaceful and happy.

coping skills (KOH-ping SKILS) Coping skills are ways of being or doing something that help manage a problem. Coping skills can help you manage anger and sadness.

emotions (i-MOH-shuns) Emotions are feelings. Anger and sadness can be strong emotions.

grief (GREEF) Grief is a feeling of deep sorrow. People feel grief when someone dies.

ignored (ig-NORD) If something is ignored, someone is paying no attention to it. You might feel sad if someone has ignored you.

irritated (IRR-i-tate-id) Someone who is irritated is mildly angry. You might feel irritated if you leave your homework behind.

rage (RAYJ) Rage is very strong, uncontrolled anger. It is difficult to calm down someone in a rage.

reacting (ree-AKT-ing) Reacting is acting or behaving in response to something. Anger can be caused by reacting to something that upset you.

resolution (rez-uh-LOO-shuhn) A resolution is something that is solved or a conflict that is worked out. Talking through something calmly can help you find a resolution.

role models (ROHL MAH-duhls) Role models are people whose good behavior should be imitated. It can help to watch how role models handle their feelings.

stress (STRES) Stress is the state of being tense or uptight caused from being upset. Feeling too much stress might make you unhappy.

tantrums (TAN-truhms) Tantrums are fits of bad temper. Toddlers throw temper tantrums.

BOOKS

Greive, Bradley Trevor. *The Blue Day Book for Kids: A Lesson in Cheering Yourself Up.* Kansas City, MO: Andrews McMeel Publishing, 2005.

Lite, Lori. *Angry Octopus: A Relaxation Story.* Marietta, GA: Stress Free Kids, 2011.

Mundy, Linus. *Being Sad When Someone Dies: A Book about Grief.* Saint Meinrad, IN: Abbey Press, 2012.

WEB SITES

Visit our Web site for links about sadness and anger:
childsworld.com/links

Note to Parents, Teachers, and Librarians:
We routinely verify our Web links to make sure they are safe and active sites. So encourage your readers to check them out!

INDEX